海军工程大学涉外丛书

外训系列教材

Chinese Martial Arts Study and Practice

中华武术学与练

主　编　徐海亮　邓　波
副主编　祝　剑　徐　青　段恪忞　卫　泽

WUHAN UNIVERSITY PRESS
武汉大学出版社

图书在版编目(CIP)数据

中华武术学与练:汉、英/徐海亮,邓波主编.—武汉:武汉大学出版社,2020.9

海军工程大学涉外丛书

ISBN 978-7-307-21605-1

Ⅰ.中… Ⅱ.①徐… ②邓… Ⅲ.武术—中国—高等学校—教材—汉、英 Ⅳ.G852

中国版本图书馆 CIP 数据核字(2020)第 107366 号

责任编辑:李 玚 责任校对:汪欣怡 版式设计:马 佳

出版发行:**武汉大学出版社** (430072 武昌 珞珈山)

(电子邮箱:cbs22@ whu.edu.cn 网址:www.wdp. com.cn)

印刷:广东虎彩云印刷有限公司

开本:720×1000 1/16 印张:13.5 字数:242 千字 插页:1

版次:2020 年 9 月第 1 版 2020 年 9 月第 1 次印刷

ISBN 978-7-307-21605-1 定价:46.00 元

前　　言

“海军工程大学涉外丛书”所属的外训系列教材是外国留学生来校学习培训的专用教材，也可作为中国军校学员专业英语培训及双语教学的辅助教材。该系列教材的逐步推出和完善，是海军工程大学对外军事教育在教学理念、教学模式和条件建设上不断努力与探索的结果，必将更好地满足外国留学生的教学需求。其主要特点是：

1. 遵循海军工程大学外训教学大纲、人才培养方案、课程教学计划和课程标准，以结构、功能、文化相结合为原则，以提高外国军事留学生的军事职业素养和专业综合技能为目标。

2. 内容的选择，强调突出各专业、各课程的知识体系及发展前沿，贴近外国军队建设和装备实际，并根据时代特点和外国军事留学生实际情况进行调整和补充，注重题材的丰富性和体裁的多样化。

3. 教材出版印刷前，均邀请校内外专家同行审阅、征求外国军事留学生修改建议，并在多年的外训教学实践中进行锤炼和检验。

《中华武术学与练》是“海军工程大学涉外丛书——外训系列教材”之一。全书共分四章，系统而简要地介绍了中华武术的历史及文化传承、特点及主要功能、基本的武术动作、武术的分类及训练方法等。可以弘扬中华传统优秀文化，使学生了解中华武术的历史与现状，掌握科学的训练方式，开阔技术视野，培养职业素养，奠定下一步专业学习的基础。

本书由徐海亮、邓波负责纲目拟定，徐青、祝剑负责全书编写统稿，段恪忞、卫泽负责全书的文稿校对、插图和数字部分的编写工作。编写过程中，参考了大量国内外文献，吸收了国内外学者的最新研究成果。在此向各位专家、学者表示衷心的感谢。书中图片均为主编组织现地拍摄。由于作者水平有限，书中难免存在疏漏和不当之处。敬请专家和读者提出宝贵意见。

编　者

2020 年 1 月

序

中华武术博大精深，以其深厚的文化底蕴和独特的魅力而深受世界人民喜爱，被誉为“人类文明流动的传奇”。她不仅是中华传统文化宝库中的奇葩，也是宣传中国传统文化的重要载体之一。对外军事培训工作是国家战略组成的重要部分，在培养国际友谊、促进合作、传播中华文化等方面都可以发挥积极的重要作用。军队院校外训工作起步于20世纪50年代，在多年的对外培训实践中，不断借助外训工作对外交往的特殊性以及宣传平台的优势，探索和完善外训课程模式，打造中国对外培训品牌。

本双语教材旨在通过中华武术向外国学员展现古老优秀的中华文明，传授知识、传播文化、增进友谊。本书从中国传统文化的角度介绍武术，通过武术课程学习，使学员在了解中华武术的同时，能切身体验到中国传统文化和现实生活的精彩；使学员熟悉掌握一些基本武术技法的同时，让他们亲身体验精神内涵和把握行之有效的训练方法；提供展示自我的舞台，在训练的过程中促进学员彼此的交流，培训学员团结协作和拼搏进取的群体精神；同时，在教学中穿插汉语文化和武德、武术精神的教育，可有效提高学员对中国传统文化的认识和汉语语言的实际运用能力。

普通高校教师和外籍教师留学生武术比赛

2016年湖北省普通高校教师和外籍教师留学生

辛勤耕
高校教师和外籍教师留学生武术比赛

Contents

Chapter 1

Introduction of Wushu

1.1 Concept of Wushu

1.1.1 The History and Culture of Wushu

Chinese Wushu (martial arts) has a long colorful history. Originally an individual combat skill, Wushu was developed by Chinese ancestors in their struggle against natural and social environments to survive. Kungfu is a colloquial term used around the world for it. Since the day it was born, Chinese Wushu has been closely connected with traditional Chinese culture. Its great inclusiveness helps to add a space of mystery and intrigue to it. Chinese Wushu has become a token of Chinese national character, revealing significant aspects of the Chinese people. With a grace that "combines the external body movements and the internal heart and soul", it has established a reputation as a valuable asset among traditional sports in the world.

Today Chinese Wushu has established a system of its own, combining the actions of kicking, striking, thrusting, etc. in a unique way to form, under standardized rules, a variety of attack and defense techniques, Tolu (a series of attack and tricks in Wushu) and forms. It is now not only very popular as an exercise for body fitting and self defense, but also highly regarded for its distinctive aesthetic value.

Wushu is a culture phenomenon. It evolves alongside the development of material and spiritual civilizations and mirrors social concepts and beliefs as they are gradually formed in people's work and military life. The cultures of different periods have left their marks in Wushu and thus these culture traits were preserved and passed down from generation to generation in a relative stable form. Throughout history Chinese Wushu has been functioning in various distinctive ways in the society.

As a cultural form, Chinese Wushu has rooted in the traditional Chinese culture. It distills the essence of Chinese philosophy, traditional regiment, combat skills and traditional aesthetic, all of those which contribute to the diversity and richness of Wushu culture. Today Chinese Wushu has become a bridge of friendship. It links the Chinese people and other countries' people and serves as a window through which the world may gain a better understanding of China radical changes have occurred to Chinese Wushu, especially in the last three decades with significant progress made to transform it into a competitive sport and to popularize it on an international level.

1.1.2 Concept of Wushu

During different times throughout history, people have different needs and perceptions about Wushu, which it is that because Wushu's development shows historical continuity and step change, and instability due to people's limited perception capacity. From the combined perspective of history and logic, Wushu's concept is a process of constant development and dynamic change. The substance, form and function of Wushu never stop developing. Due to the difference of social environment and of people's cognitive ability, the concept of Wushu is seen in various descriptions.

Nowadays, Wushu is generally defined as "a tradition Chinese sport focusing on the cultivation of physical health and spiritual power, and with combating movements as the main contents, and with Tolu, Gedou and Gong as the form of practice".

1.1.3 Wushu and Wushu Ethics

Chinese Wushu has put great emphasis on the promotion of morality. As a Wushu proverb goes, "learn morality before Wushu is ever learned, acquire". A message that's inherent in Wushu that the Wushu ethics is placed at a central position in Wushu training. Wushu ethics has a profound influence on developing a practitioner's mind, haracter, moral consciousness, and spiritual aspiration. An ideal state would be the unification of morality and skills since they are two closely related and inseparable qualities that characterize a great Wushu practitioner.

It is obvious that Wushu ethics is a common faith and a value orientation shared by Chinese Wushu practitioners from generation to generation. It is the most basic means to regulate practitioners' behavior. In the long history that Wushu culture was passed down to the later generations, Wushu ethics has fused with people's life style, mode of thinking, moral sentiments, aesthetic taste and custom. It has become an important integral part of Chinese ethics.

1.2 Characteristics and Functions

1.2.1 Characteristics of Attack and Defence

The essence of Wushu is the attacking and defending nature of the movement. The skills come from real combating. For example, both Sanda and Duanbing reflect the attacking and defending nature of Wushu. According to the sports competition rules that the principle is to avoid hurting the opponent in Wushu competition.

1. Harmonious and Integral, Physical and Spiritual—Characteristics of Wushu

The ultimate value of traditional Chinese culture lies in harmony and unity. Chinese Wushu emphasizes both standardized movements and the unity of body and spirit.

The harmony of body and spirit is a common requirement of various types and schools of Chinese Wushu. The theories of "three inner unities" and "three external unities" have been mentioned in different types and styles of Wushu. The "inner" refers to the circulation of spirit, consciousness and breath; the "external" means movements of hands, eyes, steps, etc.

All Quan's and Tolu require the harmony and unity of spirit and body movements. It reflects the fact that Wushu has been affected by ancient Chinese philosophy, medicine and esthetics during its long-term development. The unity of body and spirit is not only an issue of skills, but also the reflection of traditional Chinese culture in the form of Wushu.

2. The Richland Inclusive Content

Wushu has colorful and various contents and practice forms. Different types of Wushu have different practice methods, movement structures, skill requirements, styles and exercise load. They are suitable respectively for people of different age, gender, profession and health condition, and they are optional according to individual condition and interest. Besides, Wushu is not restricted by time, season and facilities, which is the advantageous condition for the mass of people to practice Wushu.

1.2.2 The Function of Wushu

The effect of Wushu practice is achieved by the movements of human body. Chinese people's Wushu practicing for thousands of years and scientific research have proved that Wushu exercise has various benefits to health since Wushu exercise pays attention to both physical and spiritual cultivation.

Chinese people always attach importance to exercise and health. During the development, Wushu and Chinese health preservation art have been influencing each other which strengthened Wushu's health function. Constant practicing of Wushu will benefit internal and external health. Wushu includes various forms and contents and the influences upon people's health also vary. These influences form supplements to each other, and promote health in all aspects. For instance, Changhua Tolu includes various movements such as Quashed (bending and stretching), Quichuan (curved swinging), Taoyuan (leaping), Pingheng (balancing), Fanteng(somersault), Diepu(falling), etc. These movements are beneficial to the velocity, strength, agility and endurance of human body through the concentration of attention, the coordination of breath and the participation of various body organs. Taiji and many other Wushu practices lay stress on breath and attention, and long-term practice of such Tolu will benefit on chronic illnesses and the balance of inner body environment. People can choose different Tolu or Wushu style according to their individual requirement so as to take the advantage of Wushu's function of health preserving and fulfill the purpose of health improvement.

1.2.3 The Self-defense Function of Wushu

Self-protection and self-defense is Wushu's fundamental purpose since it came into being. Even though Wushu's combat value has become less prominent than that in modern times, the combat value is still not ignorable since it is still possible that our personal safety or that of the others may be endangered in daily life. Currently the combating sport is classified as physical exercises, but the technical skills are quite close to practical corn bat and most technical actions can be directly applied in real fight. The technical methods of Tolu sports are not real fight, but the main contents are fighting and combating actions which have the functions of enhancing health level and get people familiar with certain combat skills of attacking and defending. Through such exercises, people may have command in knowledge and methods of self-defense and may strengthen some aspects of body quality and the ability to cope with unexpected incidents.

1.2.4 The Function of Education

Wushu's educational value embodies which function in school education. During the long-term development, Wushu has inherited and carried on such excellence of Chinese traditions as attaching great importance to etiquette and morality. "Being virtuous before practicing Wushu" indicates that moral education has always been emphasized during Wushu exercises. "Wushu morals" can be understood as the virtue that Wushu practitioners are required to have that refers to the spiritual system of self-control and self-discipline established by Wushu exercisers for the purpose of coping social practice and realizing their social value. Wushu morals help young people to build the virtue of respects, credit, etiquette, tolerance and self-discipline. Moreover, the exercise of Wushu requires to the spirit of endurance and perseverance, therefore Wushu exercise is beneficial for the cultivation of such virtue of indomitableness and unremitting self-improvement. Thus as an important way of morality cultivation, Wushu contributes to people's overall development. Since the establishment of the People's Republic of China, Wushu has been playing a more and more important role in school education and has made great contribution to developing campus physical activities, enriching campus culture and enhancing students' health level.

1.2.5 The Function of Entertainment and Culture Exchange

Wushu has high aesthetic value. Tolu is body and spirit rhythmic and it is the integration of It, Da, Shuai, Na, Die. All Wushu activities including every performance, competition and training which are spiritual products that serve the society. Through Wushu practicing, the contact between (connect among) countries becomes more intense. China has sent Wushu teams to other countries constantly to promote exchanging of Wushu. At the same time, more and more overseas students come to China to learn Wushu. It is obvious that Wushu plays an important role in amusement (entertainment) and cultural exchange.

1.3 The Content and Types of Wushu

Wushu is content-rich and it has many forms which have changed a lot during Wushu's process of development. By classifying Wushu's content, it is beneficial to display its basic contents that to distinguish its skill features and to reveal certain rules of Wushu and the relation between skills. There are many ways to classify Wushu. This chapter explains three types according to the forms of Wushu sport.

1.3.1 Gong

Gong focuses on single-movement practice to promote health or certain functions of the body. It can be classified into Neigong (inner Kungfu), Waging (physical Kungfu), Qinggong (light-footed Kungfu) and Rouging (flexible Kungfu).

1.3.2 Tolu

Tolu refers to the set of exercising forms derived from such combat actions which based on the contradictory variety of attack and defense, advance and retreat, movement of motive and stationary, fast and slow hollow and solid. Tolu can be divided into single-person exercise, paired exercise, and group performance.

1.3.3 Single-person Exercise

Single-person exercise is a method to practice on one's own. There are such two styles as Quanzhou (Bare-handed exercise) and Dixie (Weapon exercise) according to whether weapons are involved.

1.3.4 Quanzhou (Bare-handed Exercise)

Quanzhou refers to bare-handed Tolu exercise. Quanshu includes many types of exercises, such as Chang Quan, Nan Quan, Taiji Quan, Tingyi Quan, Baguio Zhang, Fawzi Quan, Baja Quan, Shaolin Quan, Jiangling Quan, etc.

1.3.5 Dixie (Weapon Exercise)

Weapon exercise refers to Tolu exercise with weapons. The weapons mentioned here includes long weapons, short weapons, twin weapons and soft weapons. The weapons mainly used in Wushu competitions are Dao (broad sword), Jian(sword), long cudgel, spear.

1.3.6 Paired Exercise

Paired exercise refers to the forms of Tao lug in which two or more people exercise hypothetic attacking and defending under the prearranged actions with prearrangement. Such paired exercise includes bare-handed fighting, weapon fighting and bare-handed and weapon duel.

1.3.7 Group Performance

Group performance refers to such form of Tolu exercise in which a group of people(usually 6~8 people) simultaneously practice Tolu, bare-handed, or with weapons or both. The formation of the exercise can be transformed during the exercise. A background music can be played simultaneously.

1.4 Wushu's Cultural Ideology

1.4.1 Philosophy of Chinese Wushu

Learning Wushu is more than just physical exercise, and it is necessary to understand Chinese culture, and to understand Wushu as a form of sport culture. Fighting skills are Wushu's basic elements, but Tolu, and Gong reflect the features of Chinese culture. Wushu is rich in content-rich and deep in meaning. It has the common characters of all mankind sports, and it features for the philosophical, scientific and artistic characteristics of oriental culture. Wushu is the fruit of Chinese people.

In ancient Chinese philosophy, the viewpoint of "harmony between human and heaven/nature" refers to the harmony between human and nature, human and the society, and between body and spirit. Since Wushu is the sport of human body, Wushu exercise shall abide accords with and be adaptive to the laws of nature so as to reach the unification and harmony between human and nature/universe, and to fulfill the purpose for Wushu exercise and to push for improve development. Zhou Quichuan, a renowned Chinese has mentioned "Following the heaven and learning from the field, orbicularis and hollowness are the laws of nature; hugeness and tininess will be transformed and the mystery is only acquirable by heart." His words reveal the ideology of "harmony between human and heaven/nature" and "harmony between knowledge and practice", which is Wushu's classical philosophic theory.

"The opposite is the driving force." It is the basic principle of Wushu's strategic ideology. It is the rule of sports that things will transform to the opposite side under certain come to weak, and the weak can also overcome the strong; so are the relationship between the rigid and the flexible. Chinese Wushu advocates the philosophical principle of harmony between rigidity and flexibility, and between Yin and Yang.

Chinese classical philosophy has deep influence on Wushu. The concept of Yin and Yang from the book "Yue" is the theoretical basis of Baughman. The Five-element theory is the ideological principle of Xingjian. The Tai Chi theory is the principle of Tai Chi Quan. The philosophy of Sunni has become the tactic notion of Wushu fighting. All these have proved that Chinese classical philosophy is the theoretic source of Wushu.

The super organic ancient philosophy normally accounts for a significant portion of various forms of Chinese cultural that have been inherited since ancient times. Those forms include calligraphy, music, medicine, opera, dance and Wushu, etc. They are connected with each other. Wushu combines the ideas of Yin-Yang and Five-Element from Taoism, kind heartedness from Confucianism, and tolerance from Buddhism. It also closely relates to traditional Chinese Medicine. Therefore, Wushu is more than just fighting skills, it is a complicated and organic system of constant integration and development. Without Chinese traditional culture, Wushu will not be "martial art". This is also the distinction of Wushu comparing with other foreign fighting sports of various kinds. Therefore, learning Chinese Wushu is not only learning the skills, but also the related cultural knowledge, and this makes it difficult to Chinese to learn Chinese Wushu.

1.4.2 Martial virtue of Chinese Wushu

The morals of Wushu refer to the moral principle that a Wushu exercise shall follow and the virtue that a Wushu exercise shall have during social interactions. During the development of the theory of Wushu morals, the theory of kindheartedness from Confucianism has become the basis of the traditional morals of Wushu. The basic ideas of such theory of kindheartedness of the Confucius and Mencius doctrine requires that the relationship among people shall be handled with benevolence, honesty, kindness and love. The core of Wushu morals is the unity of the exercise and the cultivation of the morality. Wushu exercise is an important method to enhance people's moral, and the exercise shall have high-level of morals and broadened mind and spirit. Wushu morals are also embodied on the application of the skills of Wushu. The nature of Wushu is fight and combat, which mean inevitable cruelty and violence. But Wushu morals emphasize making friends with Wushu, hold hand at appropriate occasion to avoid killing people. This has been required by the traditional etiquette. The Baroque (fist-clenching) Salute is a manner of Chinese traditional Wushu. Since the purpose of modern Wushu is to serve for peace and friendship, the Baroque salute has been given new meanings: the elenchid right fist represents the warrior spirit; the left palm represents the respect to virtue and making friends through Wushu competition; such four fingers of the left palm as have been put together represent the unity and progress of the Wushu field in the whole world; the curved left thumb represents an open mind to learn from pals and opponents and never to be arrogant; the bended arms represent all exercisers and schools of Wushu are like a whole family. Cherishing credit and faith, facing danger and death for kindheartedness, justice and heroic spirit are the virtue and attitude of Wushu exercisers. Being ready to help others for a just cause is an important way for Wushu exercisers to express their self-worth. Traditional wide is reach and deep in content and organ, but modern people shall carry on the positive aspect of traditional and abandon the negative aspect such as prejudice to other schools and styles, contend for orthodoxies and pushing aside dissidents, blindly following masters, doing everything good or bad for friends, etc.

1.4.3 Influence of the Difference between Traditional Chinese Culture and Western Culture

Culture is the style of ideology and behavior expressed through a nation's activities, a form that distinguishes one nation from the other. Sourced from ancient Chinese people's practice, the traditional Chinese cultures influence Chinese people's unique mode of thinking and behavior.

Traditional Chinese Wushu is a precious cultural heritage accumulated from Chinese people's long-term and continuous social practice and experience. Through thousands of years of cultural influence, Wushu has developed into a sport event with multiple functions and contents, with the theory of Chinese culture as the foundation, bare-handed or weep-on-held attacking and defending movements as the main content. Wushu boasts for its background of accumulative cultural content, unique style of actions, rich and systematic content and complicated functional structure, which western sports is not comparable. During the development for a long time, Wushu has formed its unique theory and methodology. Wushu reflects the harmony between people and nature, and between skills and morals, and this is why Wushu is popular all over the world. Wushu's world popularity is reflected in its value of physical education, i. e. it has such common characters of sports as the movements of body for health purposes. This is the significant condition for Wushu to be recognized by the world and become a part of sports. In respect of means and value, western sports focus on "practicing" and usually on overloading training; overcoming the rival is the direct goal of western sports; excitement and utilitarianism are its inherent purpose. Western sports advocate power and strength and encourage go-heads and aggressiveness. The faster and stronger shall win and the strong overcomes the weak. The symbol of success is shown through a round of victory or defeat, which demonstrates the external conquer of the power. Therefore, western sports emphasize swiftness, powerfulness and vigor; the skills and methods are relatively simply; the rules are convenient to implement; and the emphasis lies in the impact of striking. On the contrary, Wushu emphasizes on "fostering", and the combination of fostering and practice. Practice is for the purpose of "health" and "longevity". Wushu strives for stableness, self-entertaining, and security. Wushu has strong moral restrictions and many rules to shoe the qualitative factors. Being influenced by the doctrine of the mean in Chinese traditional philosophy, Wushu advocates "Do as you would be done by others" and emphasizes interior perfection and meets the requirement for self-security, and for moral and temperament cultivation. Thus, Wushu's main purpose is to realize the perfection and unity of body and spirit. The difference between western sports and Wushu is obviously seen. Compared with western athletic sports, the value of Wushu lies in its uniqueness instead of its similarity. Wushu's national character, which is indispensable for its development, is exactly the charm of Wushu. Wushu is a significant carrier of traditional Chinese culture.

Wushu should walk to the world in its own way and with its own culture characters. Modern Wushu has experienced the impact and dissimilation from western sports culture and has completed its change from pure national sport culture to the one that meets the requirement of the world and simultaneously maintains its own character. The ultimate mission of modern Wushu, which is on the way to the world, is to understand the demand of the world, to discover the highlighted point of Wushu's essence, and to attract the western people to become curious and interested in the oriental traditional culture that Wushu carries.

Chapter 2
Essential Exercises of Wushu

2.1 Exercises of Hand Forms and Strokes

2.1.1 Hand Forms

Fist: Close fingers into a fist with thumb over forefinger and middle finger.

Points to Remember: Keep the wrist unbent and hold the first tightly with the first phalanges forming a plane.

Palm: Stretch the four fingers and draw them close together while bending thumb and placing its second phalange over the palm.

Hook Hand: Bunch the five fingertips and bend the wrist.

2.1.2 Hand Method

Thrust Fist (with knuckles facing upward or sideward).

Starting Position: Stand upright with feet shoulder-width apart, fists on hips, elbows pointing backward and knuckles facing sideward.

Movements: With chest thrown out, abdomen pulled in and waist erect, thrust right fist forward forcibly, extending the right shoulder, twisting waist with a jerk and turning the right forearm inward when the right elbow moves past hip. Direct force to the foremost part of fist and straighten the arm at shoulder level. Meanwhile, pull the left elbow backward. Repeat by reversing "right" and "left".

Points to Remember: Thrust the fist with an explosive force.

2.1.3 Uphold Fist

Starting Position: The same as that for "Thrust Fist".

Movements: Move the right fist downward, leftward, upward in an arch until it comes overhead in front, with the radial side of hand facing downward. Look forward the left. Repeat by reversing "right" and "left".

Points to Remember: Relax shoulders. Bend the elbow slightly and turn the forearm inward.

2.1.4 Push Palm

Starting Position: The same as that for "Thrust Fist".

Movements: Open the right fist and thrust palm vigorously forward at shoulder level, turning forearm inward and concentrating force on the base of the palm. Meanwhile, turn the waist with a jerk and pull the left elbow backward. Repeat by reversing "right" and "left".

Points to Remember: Keep chest thrust out, abdomen drawn in and waist erect. The palm thrust should be done with an explosive force and well-coordinated with movements of the waist, shoulder and wrist. Fingers should point upward.

2.1.5 Flash Palm

Starting Position: the same as that for "Thrust Fist".

Movements: Open the right fist and move the palm sideways to the right and then upward in a curve until it comes overhead in front. Snap the wrist vigorously inward, so that the palm faces forward and the right arm is rounded. Meanwhile, turn head to the left. Keep looking at the left direction when the palm stays overhead. Repeat by reversing "right" and "left".

Points to Remember: Movements of the wrist and the head should be completed simultaneously.

2.2 Exercises of Steps and Footwork

2.2.1 Step Form

1. Bow Step

Movements: Form a left bow step, and take a big step (about 4 or 5 times the length of your foot) forward with the left foot with toes pointing slightly inward.

Bend the left leg at knee and drop to a half squat, so that thigh is almost horizontal and knee and tips of toes in a vertical line. Straighten the right leg, with toes pointing inward. Soles of both feet are placed flat on floor. Trunk is square to the front with eyes looking ahead and hands clenched into fists and placed on hips. Form a right bow step by reversing "right" and "left" in the above movements.

Points to Remember: Keep rear leg straight, chest thrust out, waist held down and hips lowered. The line between the big toe of the front foot and the heel of the rear foot should be vertical to the lateral axis of the body.

2. Horse-riding Step

Movements: Stand upright with feet about three times the length of your foot apart and toes pointing straight forward. Drop to a half squat until thighs are almost level, knees protruding no further than toes, soles flat on floor and hands clenched and placed on hips. Weight is equally distributed on both legs.

Points to Remember: Keep chest thrust out, waist held down, hips relaxed, knees turned inward and heels outward.

3. Empty Step

Movements: To form a left empty step, stand upright with hands akimbo and the left foot in front of the right. Turn the right foot 45 degrees outward and bend the right knee for a half squat while raising the left heel with toes turning slightly inward and the left leg slightly bend at knee. Your body weight is now in the rear leg. Look straight ahead. Form a right empty step by reversing "right" and "left" in the movements above.

Points to Remember: Keep chest thrust out and waist held down. To form a perfect empty step, your whole weight should rest on the rear foot.

4. Crouch Step

Movements: Stand upright with feet apart. To form a left crouch step, drop to full squat, with the right thigh resting on calf and the right foot and knee turned outward while the left leg is stretched sideways, toes pointing inward. Both soles are placed on floor and both hands are clenched into fists and placed on hips. Look straight to the left. Form a right crouch step by reversing "right" and "left" in the above movements.

Points to Remember: Keep chest thrust out and waist held down.

5. Seated Step

Movements: To form a left seared step, cross legs and drop to full squat with the left thigh resting on the right thigh and the right buttock on the raised right heel, while the left sole is placed flat on the floor with toes turned leftward. Hands are clenched and placed on hips. Look ahead to the left. Form a right seated step by reversing "right" and "left" in the above movements.

Points to Remember: Keep chest thrust out, waist held down and legs crossed tight.

6. Cross-legged Sitting

Movements: To do a left cross-legged sitting, cross your legs and sit down on the right leg which is bent at knee and placed on the floor from thigh to small toes with heel close to the left buttock, while the left leg is bent in front of the body with the left foot placed at the right side of the right thigh and the left knee kept close to chest. Hands are clenched and placed on hips. Look forward to the left. Do a right cross-legged sitting by reversing "right" and "left" in the above movements.

Points to Remember: Steps of training, common errors and corrective methods are the same as those for "Seated Step".

7. "T" Step

Movements: Stand upright with feet together. To form a left "T" step, drop to half squat with the right foot flat on floor, the left heel raised and the pointed toes of the left foot close to the arch of the right foot. The body weight is now on the right leg. Hands are clenched and placed on hips. Look straight ahead. Form a right "T" step by reversing "right" and "left" in the above movements.

Points to Remember: Steps of training, common errors and corrective methods are the same as those for "Empty Step".

2. 2. 2 Footwork

1. Beat Step

Starting Position: Stand upright with arms akimbo and with the left foot in front and shoulder-width away from the right foot.

Movements: Lean forward, lift the rear foot from the floor and make a leap forward immediately with a drive of the front leg. While in flight, beat the front foot with the rear foot. Land on the rear foot first. Look straight ahead. Repeat the movements by reversing "right" and "left".

Points to Remember: Keep trunk upright and one shoulder forward in flight.

2. Skip Step

Starting Position: The same as that for "Beat Step".

Movements: Lift the rear foot and move it towards the front foot. Skip on the sole of front foot to give way to the rear foot which should land on the sole. Bend the front leg and bring foot down in front of the rear foot. Look straight ahead.

Points to Remember: Steps of training are the same as those for "Beat Step".

3. Curved Step

Starting Position: The same as that for "Beat Step".

Movements: Drop to half squat. Stride forward in quick steps with landing foot curving round the supporting foot, each step a bit longer than shoulder-width. Look straight ahead.

Points to Remember: Keep chest thrust out and waist held clown. Maintain a well-balanced half squat position without moving the center of gravity up and down. In landing, put heel down first and then quickly place the whole sole flat on the floor. Rotate waist with every step.

2. 3 Exercises of Leg Techniques

2. 3. 1 Kick with Stretched Leg

1. Frontal Kick

Starting Position: Stand upright with feet together and arms extended sideways at shoulder level, fingers up turned or clenched into fists.

Movements: The left foot takes a half step forward. Kick with the right leg towards the forehead, ankle joint flexed. Look straight ahead. Repeat by reversing "right" and "left".

Points to Remember: Keep chest thrust out and waist erect. Keep ankle joint in flexion when you kick up and in plantar or flexion when you lower the leg. Draw in your belly forcibly and pull in your buttocks when executing the kick, which should be speeded up with explosive force when your leg reaches the waist level.

2. Oblique Kick

Starting Position: The same as that for "Frontal Kick".

Movements: The left foot takes a half step forward. Kick with the right leg towards the left ear, ankle joint flexed. Look straight ahead. Repeat by reversing "right" and "left".

Points to Remember: Steps of training, common errors and corrective methods are the same as those for "Frontal Kick".

3. Side Kick

Starting Position: Same as that for "Frontal Kick".

Movements: The left foot takes a half step forward, toes pointing outward. Raise the right heel a bit and turn trunk slightly to the left while stretching the right arm forward and the left arm backward. Kick the right foot sideways and upward towards the right ear, ankle joint dorsiflexion. At the same time, raise the left arm above the head, with the elbow slightly bent, the palm turned up and fingers pointing inward while the right forearm is placed across chest with fingers upturned or hung in front of the trunk. Look straight ahead. Do a right-side kick by reversing "right" and "left" in the above movement.

Points to Remember: Keep chest thrust out and waist erect. Turn your trunk a bit to the side of the supporting leg and draw in your abdomen vigorously while kicking.

Steps of Training: The same as those for "Frontal Kick".

4. Swing Leg Outward

Starting Position: The same as that for "Frontal Kick".

Movements: The left foot takes a half step forward to the left. Kick the right foot with leg stretched and ankle joint dorsiflexed and go upward through the left side and then bring it across the face and downward to the right side until back to the starting position. Look straight ahead. You may slap the right sole with the right palm when the right foot passes over your right shoulder. Repeat by reversing "right" and "left".

Points to Remember: Keep chest thrust out. Swing your leg in such a way as to describe a circle as big as possible.

5. Swing Leg Inward

Starting Position: The same as that for "Frontal Kick".

Movements: The left foot takes a half step forward to the left. Kick the right foot-leg stretched and ankle joint dorsiflexed upward to the right side and then bring it across the face and downward to the left side until back to the starting position. Look straight ahead. You may slap the right sole with the left palm when it passes over the left shoulder. Repeat by reversing "right" and "left".

Points to Remember: Steps of training are the same as those for "Swinging Leg Outward".

6. Kick Lower Leg with Toes Pointing Forward

Starting Position: Stand upright with feet together and arms akimbo.

Movements: Bend the right knee and raise it to the waist level with toes pointed. Kick the lower part of the right leg forward quickly concentrating force on toes. Now the right leg is straight and horizontal while the left leg may be straight or slightly bent. Look straight ahead.

Points to Remember: Keep chest thrust out, with waist erect, hips backward and toes pointed. Kick the lower leg with explosive force.

7. Kick Lower Leg with Toes Pointing Up

Starting Position: The same as that for "Kick Lower Leg with Toes Pointing Forward".

Movements: The same as those for "Kick Lower Leg with Toes Pointing Forward" except that toes are pointed upward and the kicking force is focused on heel.

Points to Remember: Steps of training, common errors and corrective methods are the same as those for "Kick Lower Leg with Toes Pointing Forward", except that toes are pointed upward.

8. Thrust Lower Leg Sideways

Starting Position: Stand upright with feet together and arms akimbo.

Movements: Place the left leg, slightly bent at knee, in front of the right leg. Straighten the left leg and lift the right knee with toes pointing inward. Thrust out the right heel forcibly sideways to shoulder level, with trunk inclining to the left. Look to the right.

Points to Remember: Focus kicking force on the heel. At the end of the movement, both legs should be straightened and the outside of instep of the kicking foot should face upward.

2.3.2 Sweeping Transformation of Leg

1. Sweep Leg Forward

Starting Position: Stand upright with feet together and arms down by at sides.

Movements: Move the left foot behind the right foot as both arms move leftward, upward and rightward in an arch until the right arm is extended sideways at shoulder level and the left hand is placed inside the right upper arm with fingers of both hands pointing upward. Look forwards to the right.

Turn about to the left as the left arm stretches out to the left side of the body until the left hand is slightly higher than shoulders. At the same time, the right arm moves horizontally in the direction of the body turn, with the palm facing forward and fingers pointing obliquely downward. Continue to turn trunk leftward with toes of the left foot pointing outward.

At the same time, the right arm moves upward, bends and moves downward with arm bent while the left arm-elbow bent and fingers pointing upward-moves upward past the inside of the right upper arm until the left palm is placed above head, facing forward.

Then put the right palm down to form a "hook hand" behind back, with fingers bunched together and pointing upward. While turning toes of the left foot outward, bend the left knee and raise the left heel. Drop to a crouch and stretch out the right leg. Using the ball of the left foot as pivot, sweep the right leg forward in a full circle with toes pointing inward and sole flat on the floor. Repeat by reversing "right" and "left".

Points to Remember: Hold head erect and truck straight. Keep looking straight ahead as the body turns. While sweeping the leg in a "crouch step", keep your balance and do not bend the outstretched leg.

2. Sweep Leg Backward

Starting Position: Stand upright with feet together and arms by sides.

Movements: The left foot takes a step forward to form a left bow step, with the left leg bent at knee and the right leg stretched. Meanwhile, thrust both palms forward at shoulder level, fingers pointing upward. Look at fingertips.

Turn toes of the left foot inward and drop the body to a full squat to form a right crouch step with the left leg bent at knee and the right leg stretched. At the same time, turn trunk to the right and bend forward, placing both palms on floor inside the right knee. Using the ball of the left foot as pivot, turn trunk rightward and sweep the right foot in the same direction in a full circle with sole flat on floor. Repeat by reversing "right" and "left".

Points to Remember: The body turns forward bending and placing of hands on floor should be done at a stretch and the movements of upper and lower limbs should be well-coordinated.

2.4 Jumping Exercises

2.4.1 Flying Kicks

Starting Position: Stand upright with feet together.

Movements: The right foot takes a step forward. Kick the left leg forward and upward and leap into the air with a drive of the right foot while swinging up both arms and striking the left palm with the back of the right-hand overhead. While in flight kick the right foot upward. Toes pointed and slap its instep with the right hand. At the same time, bend the left knee and draw the left foot to the side of the right with toes pointing downward while the left hand moves to the left side and turns into a hook slightly above shoulder level with fingers pointing downward. Trunk leans a bit forward. Look straight ahead.

Points to Remember: The right foot must go above the waist level in the upward kick. Slap the right foot when sound must be loudly and clearly. Keep your chest thrust out when leaning your trunk forward during in flight.

2.4.2 Whirlwind Steps

Starting Position: Stand upright with feet apart and palms on thighs.

Movements: Flash palm in high empty step.

Swing the right arm obliquely upward to the right and bend the left arm at the left side. Turn trunk slightly first to the right and then to the left, eyes following the right palm. Move the right palm leftward, rightward and upward in a curve until it comes overhead, where it "flashes" with a sharp dorsiflexion of wrist, so that it turns upward and fingers point leftward. At the same time, circle the left palm past the inside of the right upper arm, then overhead and to the left until the left arm extends sideways, fingers of "palm flash" at shoulder level. Place the left foot in front of the right foot to form a high empty step and toes on floor. Turn the head and eyes to the left at the same time.

2.4.3 Whirlwind Step

The left foot takes a step leftward. At the same time, swing the left hand forward and upward and the right arm backward and downward. The right foot takes a step forward, toes turned inward, ready to take off for a jump. Swing the left arm downward and bend it across the chest while swinging the right arm upward and forward. Simultaneously with arm movements, turn trunk to the left and bend forward. As weight is shifted on to the right leg, bend the right knee and leap on the right foot. Raise the left leg and swing it obliquely upward to the left, while trunk turns to the same direction. At the same time, swing both arms downward and then obliquely upward to the left. When you have completed a body turn of 360 degrees, swing the right leg upward and to the left and slap the right sole with the left palm in front of your face.

Points to Remember: While swinging the right leg upward, keep it straight and close to the chest. The swinging movement should be in a curve.

While swinging obliquely upward, the left leg should be easily extended. The left foot should take off the instant when you slap the right sole. Let it hang naturally when you are a beginner. As you become more proficient, try to raise it higher and higher and place it either straight or bent under the right thigh.

Coordinate the arm swing, take-off, kick of the right foot and the body turn which should be no less than 270 degrees.

2.4.4 Outward Leg Swing in Flight

Starting Position: Stand upright with feet together.

Movements: Stick up palms in high empty step.

The right foot draws a big step backward as the right palm swings forward and upward and the left palm swings backward. Turn the body rightward as the right arm swings upward and downward in an arch and the left arm swings forward to a position. Then turn the body back to the left as the right arm continues to swing downward and forward, and the left arm goes on moving upward and backward so that both arms come to shoulder level, with palms upturned. Simultaneously with the arm movements, shift weight on to the rear leg by pulling the left foot back to form a high empty step in front of the right foot and toes on floor. Keep chest thrusted out, waist erect and shoulders in line with arms. Eyes follow the right palm.

2.4.5 Leap in Curved Step

The left foot takes a half step forward and the right foot takes a big step obliquely forward to the right with toes pointing outward and knee slightly bent. Simultaneously with the big step, draw the right palm back to waist and swing the left hand up from behind until it comes in front of and a bit above the head. Eyes follow the right palm. Leap on the right leg while raising the left leg which is bent at knee.

At the moment of takeoff, right arm goes obliquely upward in a curve while the left arm swings to the rear. Eyes follow the right palm and then turn to the left side as you turn your head to that direction. Keep the right shoulder forward in line with the right arm. Land on the right foot and drop the left foot in front before the right foot takes a step forward, toes pointing outward. Meanwhile, turn the body rightward and lower the right arm while swinging the left arm forward.

2.4.6 Outward Leg Swing in Flight

Leap on the right foot while the left leg swings obliquely upward to the right, hands clap overhead and trunk turns to the right. Swing the right leg outward and slap instep of the right foot with the left first hand and then with the right hand while bending the left knee and pulling it to the side of the right leg. Meanwhile, lean slightly forward, eyes following hands. At the instant of slapping on the right foot, the left leg may be stretched and swung outward.

Points to Remember: The forward step should follow a curved path, the outward leg swing should follow an arch, the slaps should be loud and clear, and the takeoff and the body should be well.

Chapter 3
Introduction of Main Sort of Quan

3.1 Five-step Boxing

3.1.1 Step-by-step Teaching and Illustrations of Sets Basics

Sets practicing goes on the basis of mastering Wushu basic skills and basic sets. It is one of the major exercises for Wushu learners and also a foundation for further mastering attack and defense skills, this chapter introduces Five-step Boxing, Primary long-boxing Routine 3, Primary Broadsword Play, Primary Sword Play and Primary Cudgel accompanied with demonstration on disks to help your appreciation.

Five-step Boxing is a compiled basic set combined with the main step forms, step positions, hand forms and hand positions of Long Boxing. It is simple and easy to learn. The general requirement is standard, comfortable and strenuous in movements. The main content of the set is combinations of the five step forms: bow step, horse-riding step, crouching step, flexing footwork and cross-legged sit step; and the hand forms: brush hand thrusting fist, pressing palm, penetrating palm, blocking palm, parrying and striking, and covering with palm and striking. The whole set includes 8 movements.

3. 1. 2 Movement Names of Five-step Boxing

1. Preparatory Postures

2. Brush Hand and Punch Fist in Bow Step

3. Springing Kick and Punch Fist

4. Parrying Strike in Horse-riding Step

5. Press Palm and Punch Fist in Cross-legged Siting Step

6. Lift Knee and Penetrate Palm

7. Thrust Palm in Crouch Step

8. Block Palm in Empty Step

9. Join Feet with Fists at Waist

3.2 Longshan Shaolin Stick

3.2.1 Primary Cudgel Play

Primary Cudgel Play requires practitioners to be quick and valorous with the positions neat and determined, as the saying goes "A stick sweeps crowd". The main structure in cudgel play is made up of various cudgel positions, including cutting cudgel, circle cutting cudgel, swinging cudgel blocking cudgel, poking cudgel, pointing cudgel, bursting cudgel blocking cudgel handle, wave-circling cudgel, and step forms and positions, including bow step, horse-riding step, empty step, and S-step. The whole set contains 4 sections, 32 movements in total.

3. 2. 2 Movement Names of Primary Cudgel Play

1. Preparatory Postures

2. Join Feet and Hold Cudgel

3. Lift Cudgel Upward

4. Cut Cudgel in Bow Step

5. Cut Circling Cudgel in Bow Step

6. Swing Cudgel and Cut in Cross Step

7. Turn over, Swing Cudgel and Cut

8. Swing Cudgel Horizontal in Horse-riding Step

9. Swing Cudgel Horizontal and Cut in Jumping Step

10. Swing Cudgel and Cut with A Single Hand

11. Lift Knee and Cut Cudgel Handle

12. Swing Cudgel and Cut in Bow Step

13. Back Cudgel in Bow Step

14. Block Cudgel Handle

15. Turn Around and Poke Cudgel in Bow Step

16. Kick and Block Cudgel

17. Pull Cudgel in Bow Step

18. Lift Knee and Block Cudgel

19. Cudgel Handle and Cut in Cross Step

20. Swing Cudgel and Cut in Horse-riding Step

21. Turn over, Swing Cudgel and Cut in Horse-riding Step

22. Step Forward and Block Cudgel on Right

23. Step Forward and Block Cudgel on Left

24. Turn Around and Throw Cudgel in Crouch Step

25. Burst Cudgel in Bow Step

26. Cut Cudgel in Horse-riding Step

27. Cross Legs Sitting on Ground, Swing Cudgel Semi-circle and Cut

28. Right Horizontal Wave-circle Cudgel

29. Cross Step and Point Cudgel Downward

30. Point Cudgel Downward in Horse-riding Step

31. Poke Cudgel Downward in Cross Step

32. Lift Knee and Block Cudgel

33. Reverting Form

3.3 Nan Quan

3.3.1 Brief Introduction of Nan Quan

Nan Quan is a general designation of all sorts of Quan in various places of south China. Nan Quan has a long history, the origin can be traced back to more than 400 years ago: comparing with Quan schools in north China, it has its own features.

Nan Quan includes many styles, and they are named after their respective origin location, such as Cantonese Nan Quan, Fujian Nan Quan, etc. Nan Quan form has formed different styles and features from different geographic conditions and local cultures, for example, Guangxi Nan Quan, Zhejiang Nan Quan, Sichuan

Nan Quan, Hunan Nan Quan, Hubei Nan Quan, Jiangxi Nan Quan, etc. After the establishment of the people's Republic of China, Nan Quan was listed as one of the main events in Wushu competition in 1960. Nan Quan has been in important position in every national Wushu performance so that Nan Quan has obtained the wide development. Nan Quan is not only quite popular in China, but also has great impact on southeast countries. Nan Quan has full and solid force, so that practitioners have developed muscles and strong bones which can remarkably improve the physical quality such as power and speed, etc. Nan Quan is characterized by saving force, holding breath, giving force and voice in turns which requires abdomen breath help improving the functions of angiocarp, digesting system, respiratory system and metabolism.

1. Ready Position

2. Opening Step with Palms Thrusting

3. Feet Together Fists Clenched

4. Kylan Steps and Double Out-strike Fist

5. Bow-riding Stance Fist Punching

6. Crossing Step Flail Fist

7. Bow Step and Thrust Punch

8. Right Horizontal Nail Kick

9. Bow Stance and Thrust Punch

10. Dragon-riding Stance Fist Punching

11. Leftward Bow Stance and Thrust

12. Inserted Step Huaqiao

13. Step Elbow Press

14. Dragon-riding Stance Fist Punching

15. Open Step Double Tiger Claw

16. Dragon-riding Stance and Palm Pushing

17. Pinning Kick and Forward Falling

18. Leg Shearing

19. Carp Flip

20. Slap Ground with Feet Together

21. Single Leg Stance and Punching Fist

22. Bow Stance and down Strike Crossed First

23. Dragon-riding Stance Fist Bumping

24. Punching Fist with Feet Together

25. Bow Stance Rolling Forearm

26. Bow Stance Double Pushing

27. Bow Stance and Upper-cut Punching

28. Dragon-riding Stance Fist Bumping

29. Dragon-riding Stance Fist Punching with Step Dragging

30. Dragon-riding Stance and Finger-form Pushing

31. Kylan Steps and Double Tiger-claw Hands on Squatting

32. Closing Form

3. 4 Taiji Quan

24-form Taiji Quan is also known as simplified Taiji Quan, which is based on Yang-family Taiji Quan, and has been arranged with the principle of simplification, explicitness. It is easy to learn and exercise. Comparing to traditional Taiji Quan routines (Ta-old), the contents of 24-form are more refined, and the actions are more normative.

3. 4. 1 Movement Names

1. Commencing Form

2. Left and Right Wild Horse Splits Mane

3. White Crane Spread Its Wings

4. Left and Right Knee Brushing

5. Hand Strumming the Lute

6. Reverse Roll Forearm

7. Left Grasp the Bird' s Tail

8. Right Grasp the Bird's Tail

9. Single Whip

10. Cloud Hands

11. Single Whip

12. High Put on Horse

13. Right Heel Kicking

14. Twin Fists Strike Opponent's Ears

15. Body Turning and Left Heel Kicking

16. Left-style Crouch Down and Stand on One

17. Right-style Crouch Down and Stand on One

18. Left and Right Shuttle

19. Needle at Sea Bottom

20. Flash the Arms

21. Parry, Block and Punch

22. Apparent Close Up

23. Cross Hand

24. Closing Form

3.5 Bruce Lee's Nun Chucks

3.5.1 Practical Rod Operation

1. One-handed Shaking Stick

Preparation: Stand with your feet parallel to each other and hold your double stick with your right hand on your side. (the same as left hand movements)

Purpose: To strengthen the flexibility of the wrist through the single hand shaker. At the same time, be familiar with the feeling of holding and rotating sticks, laying a good foundation for the next basic skills.

2. The Stars Rush to the Moon

Preparation: Stand with your feet back and forth, with your right hand holding the stick, and the other side of the stick perpendicular to the ground.

Movements: The right hand hold the stick on the right side of the body, the wrist force will be the wrist as the center of rotation. One to two octaves spin backwards for 3-4 times.

Eight beats spin forward (same as the left-hand movements).

Purpose: To master the basic technical movements of the nun chucks through this section. At the same time, enhance the flexibility of the wrist, improve the ability to skillfully control the nun chucks.

3. Axillary Flowers

Preparation: Stand with your feet parallel to each other and stick under your right arm.

Movements: Raise your elbow with a right-hand stick and dial up and down with the rhythm. Lift the stick up at the forearm and then bounce down to the right armpit with the arm's elasticity. 1-4 right-hand exercises with 8 beats, 5-8 left-hand exercises with 8 beats.

Purpose: Through this section of practice, to understand the dialing force of the nun chucks, constantly enhance the flexibility of the wrist, and master the commonly used rebound parts of the nun chucks.

4. White Snakes Spit

Preparation: Stand with your right foot in front of the actual combat position, with your right hand holding the stick under right arm.

Movements:

(1) Thrust the stick forward with your right arm.

(2) At the end of the force from the bottom up in accordance with the force of the rod back, under the arm. Repeat four octaves. (the same as left hand movements)

Purpose: To improve the control ability of the nun chucks by mastering the basic forward swing.

5. Over the Range

Preparation: Stand with your feet parallel to each other, holding the upper end of the stick with your right hand perpendicular to the ground and the lower end of the stick with your left hand under your arms.

Movements:

(1) Remove the stick from the left arm under the right arm and connect the stick with the right hand under the left arm.

(2) The right hand will swing the stick from the left armpit to the right arm, while the left hand will receive the stick under the right arm.

(3) The left hand will swing the stick away from the left arm under the right arm, while the right hand will receive the stick under the left arm.

(4) The right hand will swing the stick from the left armpit to the right arm, while the left hand will receive the stick the right armpit. The last four eight beats are the same.

Purpose: To improve the flexibility of wrist and be familiar with stick.

6. Suqin Bears Sword

Preparation: Stand with your feet parallel to each other, stick around 45 degrees behind you and the ground, holding the upper end of the stick with your left hand and the lower end of the stick with your right hand.

Movements:

(1) Stroke the stick from the bottom to the top half circle from behind, swing the stick to the left arm, and connect the stick with the right hand below. Hand the

stick from the bottom to the top half circle from behind, swing the stick to the right arm, while the left hand receives the stick below.

(2) Stroke the stick from the bottom to the top half circle from behind, swing the stick to the left arm, and connect the stick with the right hand below.

(3) Stroke the stick from the bottom to the top half circle from behind, swing the stick to the right arm, and connect the stick with the left hand below. The last four eight beats are the same.

Purpose: To improve the flexibility of wrist and be familiar with stick.

7. Travel Far and Wide

Preparation: Stand with your feet parallel to each other, holding the upper end of the stick with your right hand perpendicular to the ground and the lower end of the stick with your left hand under your armpits.

Movements:

(1) The left hand will swing the stick from the left arm under the right arm, while the right hand will receive the stick under the left arm.

(2) The right hand will swing the stick from under the left arm to the right arm, while the left hand will receive the stick under the right arm.

(3) The stick is removed from the left arm under the right arm, while the right hand receives the stick behind.

(4) Half circle the stick from the bottom to the top with the right hand, swing the stick to the right arm, and connect the stick with the left hand below. The last four eight beats are the same.

Purpose: To improve the flexibility of wrist and be familiar with stick.

8. Sweep the Enemy

Preparation: Right foot is in front, stands in actual combat position step, right hand holds a stick, the other side of the stick is clamped in right armpit.

Movements:

(1) Turn the side clockwise once. Then rotate the stick counterclockwise to the right.

(2) Right hand sweep stick.

(3) Put the stick under your right arm and return to the ready position. The last four eight beats are the same.

Purpose: To improve the flexibility of wrist and be familiar with stick.

3. 5. 2 Sets of Practical Rod Exercises

1. Three Stars Raises the Sun

Preparation: Right foot is in front, stands in actual combat position step, right hand holds a stick, stick one end clip in right armpit.

(1) Hold the stick under the arm in the left hand, lift the stick, turn the head counterclockwise from front to back, and sweep the stick to the left side of the body vigorously.

(2) Connect the stick with your left hand on the left, then sweep the stick to the right.

(3) The right hand takes the stick on the right, then sweeps it to the left.

(4) The left hand takes the stick on the right, then sweeps it to the right.

(5) The right hand takes the stick on the right side, slams it to the front, carries it under the left arm.

(6) The right hand slams the stick to the front from the left arm, carries it under the right arm.

(7) The left hand takes the stick from the right arm, slams it to the front, carries it under the left arm.

(8) The right hand takes the stick from the left arm, slams it to the front, carries it under the right arm.

Purpose: This type consists of a sweeping stick and a splitting stick. It mainly attacks the sides and head of the enemy's body. At the same time, it can train the coordinate ability of the left and right arm.

2. Unbeatable Spin

Preparation: The right foot is in front and stands in actual combat position position. The right Suqin bears sword (the stick is placed vertically on the ground. The right hand holds the upper end of the stick, the left hand holds the other end of the stick under the right arm).

(1) The right hand slams the stick to the front.

(2) Lift the stick and return to the first position.

(3) Slam the stick to the left side and make a clockwise revolution.

(4) The left hand pulls the stick to the right and make an anticlockwise revolution.

(5) Reverse the right wrist, pull the stick to the right and make a clockwise revolution.

(6) The right hand holds the stick and pulls it to the right, make a anticlockwise revolution and make a downward strike.

(7) Lift the stick and hold it on right arm.

(8) Hold the stick under the right arm quickly from upside to downside.

Purpose: This type is aimed at training the coordination and flexibility of the stick and the whole body. It is used to strike the people in front and confuse the rivals.

3. Movements Against Tiger

Preparation: The right foot is in front and stands in actual combat position. Use right Suqin bears sword position.

(1) The right hand holds the stick, slams it from the upper right to lower left violently.

(2) Lift it to upper left and slams it to lower right violently.

(3) Return to right Suqin bears sword position.

(4) Pat the inner side of the right leg from up to down and uplift the leg at same time.

(5) Make a clockwise revolution after the rebound.

(6) Take the stick to left hand under the hip.

(7) Return to left Suqin bears sword position when foot falls to the ground.

(8) Change to right Suqin position.

4. River Flowing

Preparation: The right foot is in front and stands in actual combat position. The right-hand acts as a snake reach out its tongue. (The right hands hold the stick and the other end of the stick is under the right arm.)

(1) Sweep the stick to the right.

(2) The right hand holds the stick and makes a spin around the body from the left to right.

(3) Make a spin around the body from the right to left.

(4) The right hand holds the stick and makes a spin around the body from the left to right, the right hand takes the stick behind the body at the same time.

(5) The left hand holds the stick and seeps it to the right.

(6) The left hand takes the stick and makes a spin around the body from the right to left.

(7) Makes a spin around the body from the left to right.

(8) The left hand holds the stick under the left arm.

Purpose: Be more familiar with the stick through the practice.

5. Wings up

Preparation: Stand in parallel, right Suqin bears sword position.

(1) The right hand holds the stick and split from up to lower left.

(2) The stick draws a half circle counterclockwise on the left side of the body, then hits from the upper left to the lower right.

(3) Crow the stick on the right arm.

(4) The right hand holds the stick to the left and hits it, the left hand touches the stick on the shoulder.

(5) After the left-hand stick, go from the top to the bottom right.

(6) Then draw a half circle counterclockwise on the right side of the body, from top right to bottom left.

(7) Lift the stick upwards on the left arm.

(8) The left hand holds the stick to the right and the other slams and the right hand touches the stick on the shoulder.

Purpose: Based on the familiarity of the stick, training the ability of the back stick to achieve the goal of enhancing the overall control stick.

6. Buddha Light Top

Preparation: Right foot in front, performing like right Suqin position.

(1) Swing the stick to the top of the head and rotate clockwise around the top of the head.

(2) Put the stick to the same height as the abdomen and rotated counter-clockwise one full turn.

(3) Waving above the head and swinging to the lower left.

(4) Pull the stick back to the top of the head and turn it counterclockwise around the top of the head.

(5) Pull to the abdomen position and rotate clockwise.

(6) Pull the stick to the lower right side of the body and then tap it to the upper left.

(7) Attack from the upper left to the lower right.

(8) Back to the posture of right Suqin sword style.

Purpose: Improve the control of sticks and familiarize them with sticks in the body.

7. Fortune

Preparation: Two feet stand in parallel, right crutch.

(1) Right hand sweeping stick to the left.

(2) Sweep the stick to the right and stick the left hand at the same time.

(3) The left hand sweeps the stick to the right.

(4) Then the left hand sweeps the stick to the left behind and the right hand takes over the stick.

(5) Right hand swings the stick to right arm.

(6) To the lower left, fiercely beat the stick.

(7) Hold the stick with your left hand and swing it to the left arm.

(8) Fight straight ahead and close on the left side.

Objective: To strengthen the flexibility of the wrist and the ability of the two hands to receive the stick.

8. Overturning the Sea

Preparation: The right foot stands in front and stands in actual combat steps and becomes the right Suqin bears sword position.

(1) The right hand rotates the stick one clockwise to the left.

(2) Then rotate the stick one counterclockwise to the right.

(3) Fight the stick down.

(4) Pick the right hand wrist and play the other side of the stick from the bottom up to the left hand.

(5) Raise the stick with both hands, and then use your right hand to slam the stick to the lower left.

(6) Shake the wrist with your right hand, and rotate the stick two turns from the bottom up to the right arm.

(7) Then right hand hold the stick under the right armpit.

(8) Receiving the stick into the right Suqin bears sword position.

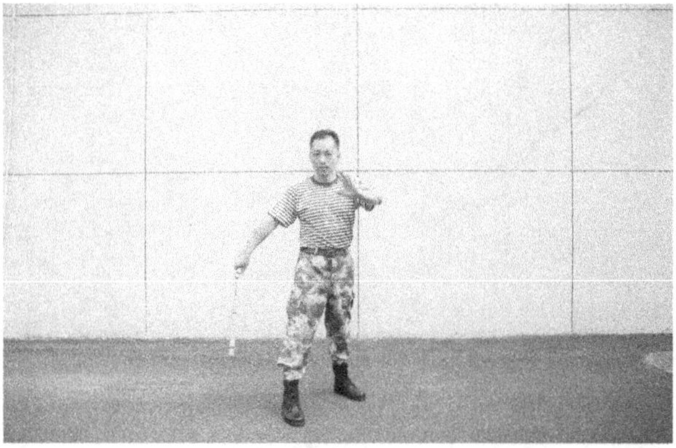

Purpose: To strengthen the flexibility of the wrist and the ability of the two hands to receive the stick.

3.5.3 Practical Nunchaku of Special Forces

1. Preparations

Stand in position, merge the nunchaku and inserted at the back right waist belt.

Purposes: Carry concealed and easy to hit out.

2. Preparatory Potential

On the basis of the preparation posture, hear the "nunchaku" password, quickly right pendulum head, toes close, visual right waist, while both hands clap grip nunchaku. Hear "preparation", both hands pull the stick together, while the body left the left foot into a virtual step, hands horizontal stick forward with the chest with high, visual front.

Purposes: This is a practical nunchaku routine appearance of the action, the performance process of the main emphasis on the movement in place and neat.

3. The First Potential: The Immortal Point of the Road

Movements: Hand in hand with the stick to the right, move forward the center of body weight to the right foot. With the right hand, clamp the bottom of the stick with thumb and palm inner edge, send out the nunchaku that rest on the top of the button horizontally with a short and smashing power, force up to the end of the stick. After the force to the tip of the homeopathic forward after the stick, turn it three weeks, put the stick in the right armpit. At this time, set the left hand palm up to defense body, the body slightly turn left side forward, slightly to the right empty stance.

Purposes: This potential is mainly used to take advantage of the enemy's unprepared or neglect of facial defense, click enemies face, head, eyes and other parts, to cause severe damage to enemy unexpected.

4. The Second Potential: White Snake Spit Letter

Movements: The right foot moves forward two times in succession, loosens the armpit instantly when upper the step, the arm extends the right wrist quickly to make the strength, will the stick to the left and the lower right below the hard chop. Using the strength of the arm, pull the stick back to the right arm, the left hand grip stick in the armpit, into actual combat steps.

Purposes: This potential is a very practical moves. Can be used in actual combat position to attack the enemy's head, face, shoulder, jaw, chest and low bow and other parts, because it is fast, strength enough, it is more difficult to be cracked by the enemy.

5. The Third Potential: Sweeping the Top Knee

Movements: Loosen the left hand stick, the body quickly left stare into the left lunge, right hand with a stick to the left with a violent sweep, left hand on the left side of the stick, hands horizontal stick to the left thigh. At this time the stick body level, slightly with the legs into a cross. Right pedal into the right lunge, the hands horizontal stick forward square block, homeopathy up the left pedal to the top knee.

Purposes: This potential sweeping stick action is used for transverse sweep, force reach the end of the stick, mainly hit the enemy cheek, temples and other parts. Top knee used in close combat, according to actual situation with the stick chain block enemy under the attack and then knee back to its waist and abdomen, or with the rod chain quickly hang the other side of the neck pull off the top knee, to hit the enemy's goal.

6. The Forth Potential: Turn Around and Split the Stick

Movements: Left foot drop step to the right, the body quickly turn right, the right foot fell step and right hand stick straight downward split. Force to the end, the wrist will be picked on the stick, the left hand behind the stick into a back sword style. This is the actual combat steps.

Purposes: The potential used to attack the enemy quickly through a sudden change in stature. Split upright downward, the hit site is mainly head, shoulder, or armed hands.

7. The Fifth Potential: Stick Pedal

Movements: When the left foot is kneeling step to the left front, quickly dives the center of body weight, grip sticks from right to left violently sweeps the enemy leg with right hand. The left hand on the body side stick up to the rack block, protect the head. At the same time up the right foot pedal.

Purposes: This potential in combat with a stick to the enemy below the knee of the leg, so that the enemy instantaneous loss of combat effectiveness. When the enemy dodge counterattack, stick defense and use the kick to hit the enemy's chest and abdomen.

8. The Sixth Potential: Over the Range

Movements: Immediately afterwards, steps forward with right foot and beat with right stick. After the force is exhausted, pick the stick to the right arm and the left hand to the other stick from the right. Then he takes a big step forward with his left foot. At the same time, the left-hand stick slams from the bottom to the top and then withdraws left arm. The right hand holds the stick on the left and the back. When the body is turned to the right, the right-hand stick sweeps from the waist to the right and back, and the wrist turns the force. The left hand grips the stick behind. At this point, the stick is placed behind the back and the body faces the right side into a horse-studded style.

Purposes: This trend is mainly composed of three common hitting movements such as squatting, smashing and sweeping. Through the cooperation of footwork, the enemy can conduct continuous multi-directional and multi-part attacks to achieve an attack effect that is untenable for the enemy.

9. The Seventh Potential: Snowflakes

Movement: After stepping forward with right ankle, swing club counterclockwise for three weeks on the top of his head, sweep the force from top to bottom, and left hand is on the left waist (the first move of the third trend). At this point, two hands are placed on the thighs on the left side of the body and become horses.

Purposes: This potential is mainly used to protect the head and wait for an opportunity to attack the enemy's temples, cheeks and other parts.

10. The Eighth Potential: The Side Stick

Movements: While left-handed to give the right hand to the stick, left foot to

the right step, left foot side. After turning left, the left foot turned to the left, took a fist with his left hand and held the stick with his right hand. He opened it into a fighting preparation.

Purposes: This potential is used in the combined use of stick and leg methods in actual combat position to attack the enemy in the best way.

11. The Ninth Potential: Straight Punching Stick

Movement: After a small step left jab on the left foot, the body borrowed the force to the left, and the right hand held the stick with a nunchaku stick to the lower left obliquely. At this point, the left hand fist head, right hand grip stick slightly oblique, into real combat.

Purposes: This trend is mainly used in close combat, with a single (overlapping) club stick end of the enemy ribs, waist slamming. Give full play to the unique, flexible, concise, sudden and changeable technical features to quickly subdue the enemy.

12. The Tenth Potential: Call Crowbar

Movements: Turn your right arm down and turn your wrist to make a quick call. Move your right foot forward and step up to the left to get a crowbar. At this time, the palm of the left hand is placed on the chest and the body is slightly shifted to the right.

Purposes: This trend is mainly aimed at armored enemies from the following stabbed, oblique thorns, provocations and other attacks attack interception, the main hitting position is the enemy armed wrists, arms. If the enemy resorts to dodging by means of acrobatic strides, it will quickly cooperate with successive moves such as cymbals and cymbals to achieve the ultimate goal of subduing the enemy.

13. The Eleventh Potential: Counterattack with Whip Leg

Movements: The right-hand stick made a round clockwise rotation on the head from the kneeling down to the upper right, closing the stick to the right. The body turned to the right, whip your left foot to quickly fall. At this point, the left hand has become a real combat position.

Purposes: This trend is mainly used to attack the enemy by using a stick to rotate when the enemy is attacked by my arm and leg. The movement range is small, the speed is fast, and the counter-attack movement is easy to connect. Quickly whip up after the block, you can hit the opponent's leg, waist and head in real combat. This is a typical defensive counterattack combination.

14. The Twelfth Potential: Horse-stance Stick Split

Movements: The right hand stick quickly sideways downward split dozen, take the left foot step on the same time to sweep the stick to the left, the left hand in the chest block, right foot before the right dodged, turn the wrist will stick to pick, the left hand horizontal palm down, slightly sideways into kneeling.

Purposes: This potential is split roll, sweep stick action small combination, mainly used in the continuous beating behind, do not give the enemy the opportunity to breathe, the use of easy connection, easy to force the characteristics of the enemy to hit.

15. The Thirteenth Potential: Pick up the Steps on Your Knees

Movements: The right hand stick quickly sideways downward split dozen, take the left foot step on the same time to sweep the stick to the left, the left hand in the chest block, right foot before the right dodged, turn the wrist will stick to pick, the left hand horizontal palm down, slightly sideways into kneeling step.

Purposes: This potential is in conjunction with the footwork on the basis of a flexible application of enemy attacks based on footwork and body dodge, while defending counterattack. The stick is mainly used to hit the jaws and other parts of enemies.

16. The Fourteenth Potential: Standing Stick Block

Movements: Right pedal ground up, left foot step forward, while right hand to the right arm to send the stick on the left shoulder. The right foot is pulled to the right and the right hand grip is struck to the right. Pull the left hand back to the grip, the body turned right stare into a lunge, the right hand turned about with the eyes with high left hand in the next, quickly set up a stick to the outside block.

Purposes: This potential for the basic defensive action, the use of the middle of the stick chain of two sticks to attack the enemy to the upward or outward block defense. Attention to the attack action of the combination of the actual and the attack and defense of the combination of the speed and strength of the block action.

17. The Fifteenth Potential: Transverse Da Yu Split

Movements: The left foot quickly left the front step, the right hand grip sticks with the stick tip to the left blows the enemy head. Follow up on the right foot, and the right stick splits against the right. Pull the stick back after the force is done, and flip it over the top of the head and close the stick to the right armpit. At this time, the left hand in front of the chest of eight feet, sideways into a horse stance.

Purposes: This potential is mainly in the near-body combat, when the two-section stick can not be expanded in time to apply. To strike the head, face, and jaw of an enemy with a stick tip. Should pay attention to the use of the power to turn the waist, quick bash, to hit the enemy's effect.

18. The Sixteenth Potential: Dragon Pendulum Its' Tail

Movements: The body turns left and the right stick is pulled straight from the armpit to the left and quickly back behind. At this time the wrist will be a stick to return before, skillful force pull recovery grip stick in the right hand to protect the cheek, while the left hand horizontal palm slightly down, into a horse stance.

Purposes: This potential for the body side of the crotch of the opponent to hit, emphasizing the wrist to the flexible control of the stick, the size of dodge and the club to ease.

19. Collect Potential

The body center of gravity left, the right hand grip stick, the left hand clenched, at the same time close to the waist. Set up a positive posture by foot.

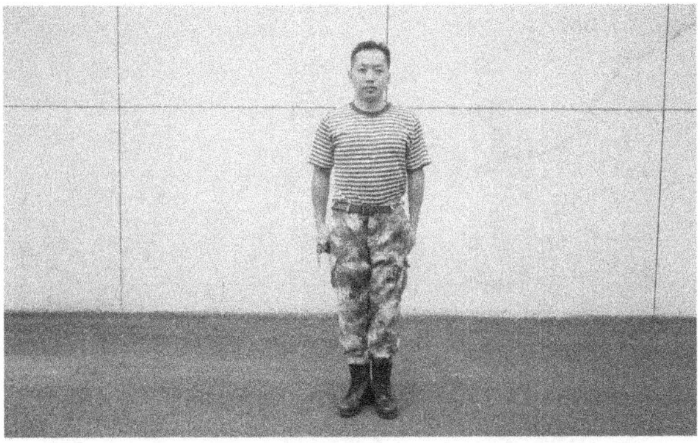

3.6 PLA's Sports Boxing

Martial body boxing is a combination of boxing, foot kicking, wrestling, knife grabbing and gun grabbing. It is of great importance to carry out military physical boxing training on a regular basis to cultivate the style of fighting with perseverance and courage.

In the coming war, we are facing a fierce enemy, not a lamb who will die with his hands tied. In carrying out special missions such as reconnaissance, anti-submarine, reconnaissance and camouflage, as well as brave and righteous actions to protect the legitimate interests of the people from aggression, we often have to confront the enemy with our bare hands.

3.6.1 Preliminary Pose

1. Preliminary pose 1

2. Preliminary Pose 2

3. Preliminary Pose 3

4. Preliminary Pose (Side Vision)

3.6.2 Stumble Leg Pressure Elbow

1. Stumble Leg Pressure Elbow 1

2. Stumble Leg Pressure Elbow 2

3. Stumble Leg Pressure Elbow (Side Vision)

4. Stumble Leg Pressure Elbow 3

5. Stumble Leg Pressure Elbow 4

6. Stumble Leg Pressure Elbow 5

3.6.3 Lunges Hit Elbow

1. Lunges Hit Elbow (Side Vision 1)

2. Lunges Hit Elbow (Side Vision 2)

3. Lunges Hit Elbow 1

4. Lunges Hit Elbow 2

3.6.4 Chops Ribs Under

1. Chops Ribs Under 1

2. Chops Ribs Under 2

3. Chops Ribs Under 3

4. Chops Ribs Under 4

5. Chops Ribs Under 4 (Side Vision)

3.6.5 Step Forward and Flick Your Arm

1. Step Forward and Flick Your Arm 1

2. Step Forward and Flick Your Arm (Side Vision)

3. Step Forward and Flick Your Arm 2

4. Step Forward and Flick Your Arm(Side Vision)

5. Step Forward and Flick Your Arm 3

6. Step Forward and Flick Your Arm(Reverse Side)

3. 6. 6 Double Punch and Then Attack

1. Double Punch and Then Attack 1

2. Double Punch and Then Attack 2

3. Double Punch and Then Attack 3

4. Double Punch and Then Attack 4

5. Double Punch and Then Attack 5

3. 6. 7 Precaution the Left Legs

1. Precaution the Left Legs 1

2. Precaution the Left Legs 2

3. Precaution the Left Legs 3

4. Precaution the Left Legs 4

3.6.8 Choke the Neck and Throw it Down

1. Choke the Neck and Throw it Down 1

2. Choke the Neck and Throw it Down (Side Vision)

3. Choke the Neck and Throw it Down 2

3. 6. 9 Greg Strike

1. Greg Strike 1

2. Greg Strike(Side Vision)

3. Greg Strike 2

3. 6. 10 Prevent Right Fist

1. Prevent Right Fist 1

2. Prevent Right Fist 2

3. Prevent Right Fist 3

4. Prevent Right Fist 4

3.6.11 Stop the Attack and Hold the Legs

1. Stop the Attack and Hold the Legs 1

2. Stop the Attack and Hold the Legs 2

3.6.12 Lift the Thigh and Lock Throat

1. Lift the Thigh and Lock Throat 1

2. Lift the Thigh and Lock Throat 2

3. Lift the Thigh and Lock Throat 3

3. 6. 13 Heel Kick and Horizontal Hook

1. Heel Kick and Horizontal Hook 1

2. Heel Kick and Horizontal Hook 2

3. Heel Kick and Horizontal Hook 3

4. Heel Kick and Horizontal Hook 4

3.6.14 Take A Step Forward and Catch Your Leg

1. Take A Step Forward and Catch Your Leg 1

2. Take A Step Forward and Catch Your Leg 2

3.6.15 Tripping the Tripping Leg

1. Tripping the Tripping Leg 1

2. Tripping the Tripping Leg 2

3. Tripping the Tripping Leg 3

4. Tripping the Tripping Leg 4

5. Tripping the Tripping Leg 5

6. Tripping the Tripping Leg (Side Vision)

3.6.16 Bow Up

1. Bow Up 1

2. Receive Power (End 1)

3. Bow Up 2

4. Receive Power (End 2)

Chapter 4

Teaching and Training Demonstration of Routine

4.1 Teaching and Training Principles

4.1.1 Principles of Motivation and Interest

To learn Wushu, the learner must have a correct intention and attitude, and evolve direct interest into indirect interest. Teacher should help erect right intention and attitude in every class and mobilize learners' motivation.

4.1.2 Principle of Flexible Treatment

Learners differ in aspects of physical quality, sex, age and so on, so may differ in learning rapidity and effect. In teaching, teacher must deal with them accordingly. For example, in content selection, choose more force and speed demanding contents for male learners, and choose more grace and flexibility related contents for female learners.

4.1.3 Principle of Systematic Teaching

Teaching of routines must start with basic work and be conducted systematically from simple contents to difficult contents, from basic movements to various forms and positions: step forms, step positions, hand forms and hand positions, then to jumps and balancing, and finally the whole routine. Gradually pursue the natural combination of hand, eyes, body step, spirit, breath, force and power and perfection of learners' practicing of Wushu techniques.

4. 1. 4 Principle of Consolidation and Improvement

"Thousands of blows bring perfection of Wushu" After class teaching, ask learners to keep exercising and continuously give them new and higher requirements. The taught movement should become dynamically fixed, and be improved gradually. For example, in learning "flying kick", may first teach jump on one foot, with the other foot landing first, then teach jump on one foot with both feet landing together, and at last jump on both feet with both feet landing at the same time.

4. 1. 5 Principle of Secularity and Periodicity

Power practicing demands three times one day, tree rounds one time, where one missing may lead to all lost. Keep exercising despite conditions At the same time arrange exercise by cycles. This is a very important Wushu teaching principle. Persistence guarantees consolidation and improvement of skills, and cultivation of will strength; on the basis of long term persistence, cycles are set as long as years and as short as one year or one month. Exercising contents and workout loads are different in different types. This guarantees systematic training in the long run.

4. 1. 6 Principle of All-round Training and Specific Training

Combine all-round training and specific training. Without all-round development of physical quality as the base, one can never raise his/her Wushu standard. At every stage, especially at the early stages, all-round training should be given adequate attention. All-round training and specific training are complementary in effect. So they should be well arranged and not be isolated or biased.

4. 1. 7 Principle of Set-plus Training

Routine sets practicing requires as its basic conditions the quality of adequate speed, endurance, force and flexibility. Therefore in everyday training, workout load should be sufficient. The method of practicing whole routine set plus half or some sections of it can be employed, which helps to increase training intensity and physical power needed for completion of the routine.

4.2 Notes for Teaching and Training

4.2.1 Employment of Teaching Methods

Teaching methods for Wushu generally includes lecture, whole movement teaching and movement decomposition prevention and correction. Employ exercise, competition, and appropriate methods to achieve good result. In lecturing, explain less and exercise more, in vivid language so that learners may not feel insipid and may get a clear understanding of the technical tips. Teacher should also ask learners to set positive attitude. In demonstration, oral instruction is secondary to demonstration and imitation. In exercising, class work is primary, and work in rows is secondary, so as to ensure the workout load and intensity.

4.2.2 Make Clear of Teaching Stages

Follow the principle of gradualness, i. e. from easy to difficult, from shallow to deep. Only after having taught basic work, basic movements and teach the basic rout basic combinations, can teacher continue. Weapon routine is taught after boxing routines. Duel and combat are to be practiced only after the consolidation and improvement of routines by singles.

4.2.3 Divide Teaching Steps Clearly

Wushu routines are made up of multiple movements, including movement route, parrying structure, force exertion, and so on. To accomplish teaching tasks, procedures should be arranged orderly, every step known clearly by learners, so that learners may eventually learn every movement and grasp whole style of the routine. Step one, make clear of them movement route. Step two, require learners to grasp postures accurately and neatly. Step three, require learners to do movement smoothly. Step four, analyze force exertion. And step five, review.

4.2.4 Arrange Teaching Materials Properly

Wushu contains lots of step forms and positions, so lower limbs may bear much pressure. It is ideal that there are two teaching stuffs, with one focusing on upper limbs. In that case, learners can get trained all-around and also more can be acquired.

4. 2. 5 Cultivate Teaching Backbones

Choose some outstanding and active learners to study in advance so that in class they can assist teacher. In class, find outstanding learners to be the backbones to assist teacher's instruction. For example, in group work ask backbones to demonstrate and lead other learners, standing at different points.

4. 2. 6 Make Good Use of warm-ups

Warm-up is done in every class. According to teaching content of class include some basic and regular movements in specific warm-up, like fist holding, fist thrusting, etc., so that teaching can benefit from both time-saving and smooth transition.

4. 3 Structural Analysis on Teaching and Training

The structure of basic routine teaching generally includes warm-up main part and cool down. Warm-up includes general activities and specific activities. It is a preparation for the teaching and training in the main part. Main part, as the core of a class, is the main teaching and training content cool-down part is the closing of a class. It is to relax the body, consolidate the teaching and training contents and prepare for the next class.

The teaching contents, key teaching points, difficult points, organization teaching as well as the workout load should all be written in detail in teaching. For example, for a class on "Flying kick" of Primary Long Boxing Routine 3 Section 4, in the warm-up, some movements related to it such as jumping, foot patting, the form off ground, fist punch in cross-legged step, etc. should be included so as to facilitate the completion of the main content. Besides, in cool-down, the parts of lower limbs and waist should be relaxed particularly because in exercising "Flying kick" the lower limbs and waist bear more pressure and get more fatigued than other parts of the body.

4.4 Teaching and Training Arrangements of Routine Sets Basics

The following teaching and training arrangements are for teacher's and learners' reference and convenience.

4.4.1 Warm-up Part

General warm-up. (sixteen times).
Neck movements.
Shoulder movements.
Chest out movements.
Body press side movements.
Turn body movements.

4.4.2 Specific Warm-up (Sixteen Times)

Stake standing.
Punch fist in shoulder-width stance.
Punch fist in horse-riding step.
Changes in hand forms.
Punch fist in horse riding step.
Punch fist in bow step.
Swing arms in crouching step.
Leg stretch in bow step.
Leg stretch in crouching step.
Press leg forward with bending trunk.
Press leg forward with mouth to the toe.
Side leg stretch.
Side split.
Parallel-split.
Front tap foot.
Hold leg left and right.
Raise knee and charge leg.
Back bend.

Circle trunk with arms s weeping.

4.4.3 Main Part

1. Exercise in Kicks(eight times)

Front kick.

Cross kick.

Side kick.

Kick-circle Inward.

Kick-circle outward.

Back kick.

2. Hit Sound Leg Position(eight times)

Front tap foot.

Kick-circle inward with tap foot.

Kick-circle outward with tap foot.

3. Leg Flex and Extend(eight times)

Snap kick and punch fist.

Heel kick and push palm.

Side sole kick.

4. Basic Movements(four times)

Swing arms and tap leg.

Pierce palm in crouch step.

Turn waist over in back-cross step.

Swing arms and turn waist over.

Front sweep.

Back sweep.

Arc step.

5. Jump Movements(four times)

Taking-off.

Turn body over from horse step.

Jumping outside kick.

Giant leap.

Flying kick.

Whirlwind kick.

kick-flight as waving lotus.

Side somersault.

Butterfly.

Jumping-turning body 360°.

6. Exercise on Routine: A Boxing Routine and A Weapon Routine Exercise Mixed

(1) Primary boxing routine 3 (or five step boxing).

Three times for class work, three times in groups, class competition once.

(2) Primary broad sword or primary sword, or primary cudgel play.

Three times for class work, three times in groups, class competition once.

7. Cool Down Part

Stand upside down (sixteen times).

Beat arms and rap legs (sixteen times).

Common Expressions Terms of Formation

一、队列队形集合 Terms of Formation

1. 立正!
   Attention!
2. 稍息!
   Stand at ease!
3. 向右(左)看齐!
   Eyes right(left)!
4. 向前看!
   Eyes front!
5. 向中看齐!
   Guide centre!
6. 报数!
   Count off!
7. 一、二报数!
   By twos number!
8. 靠拢!
   Close!
9. 散开!
   Extend!
10. 齐步走!
    Quick step(march)!
11. 便步走!
    At ease march!
12. 跑步!

On the double!

13. 换步!

Get step!

14. 坐下!

Sit down!

15. 解散!

Dismiss!

16. 向后转!

About face(turn)!

17. 向右(左)转!

Right(Let)face(urm)!

18. 踏步,走!

Mark time, march!

19. 出列!

Out of ranks! Fall out to me!

20, 向前三步,走!

Three steps forward, march!

21. 左(右)为准!

Guide. left(right)

22. 以我为准!

Guide on me!

23. 前后离开一步!

Open rank!

24. 向前靠拢!

Close ranks!

25. 蹲下!

Squat down!

26. 站队!

Line up(Stand in line)!

27. 点名!

Roll Call!

二、教学训练 Teaching and Training

1. 到上课时间了。
   lt' s time for class.
2. 现在，我们开始上课。
   Now, let' s begin our class.
3. 今天，我们教学《武术基础功》课程。
   Today, let's start the course of *The Basic Skills of Wushu*.
4. 现在，我们教学"马步冲拳"，请看完整示范。
   Now, let's learn punching fist in horse-riding step. Please watch the complete demonstration.
5. 下面，我们进行分解教学。
   Now, let's step by step.
6. 请再看一次。
   Watch it again.
7. 请跟我学。
   Follow me, please.
8. 请听口令做练习，一、二、三、四、五、六、七、八！
   One, two three, four, five six, seven, eight. Please follow me with the exercises.
9. 重做一遍。
   Once more.
10. 好！今天我们的课就上到这里，同学们再见！
    Ok, time is up. Goodbye, everyone.
11. 今天，我们训练的主要内容：一是练习武术基本功；二是复习组合动作；三是整理放松。
    Today, we have the following main contents: firstly, practicing the basic skills of Wushu; secondly, review the integrated movements; thirdly, relaxing exercise.
12. 首先，我们做准备活动。
    Now, let's do warm-up.
13. 先做一般性准备活动，再做专项性准备活动。
    First, the general, then, we have some special exercises.

14. 请大家站成两排，我们做定位操练习。

Please stand in two lines: here comes orientation exercises.

15. 请大家站成两路纵队，我们做行进间的练习。

Please stand in two rows: we are going to do marching forward.

16. 下面，我们做“踢腿”练习。

Next, we are learning kicking leg.

17. 请大家一个跟一个做练习。

Please do it one by one.

18. 请大家跟着我做练习。

Please follow me.

19. 请大家集体演练一遍。

Let's do it all together.

20. 下面，我们进行分组练习。第一组，练习“仆步抡拍”60 个；第二组，练习“腾空飞脚”20 个。

Next is group practice. For the first group, swing arms in crouch step 60 times; the second group, flying kick, 20 times.

21. 眼随右拳。

Eyes following the right fist.

22. 外练筋骨皮，内练一口气。

The outside practice of bones, muscles, skin, and inside training in one breath.

23. 内外合一，神形兼备。

Pay attention to internal and external, form and spiritual combination.

24. 目视前方。

Eyes looking ahead.

25. 身体右转。

Turn the body to the right.

26. 好，今天我们训练到此结束！再见！

Well, that is all for today. Bye-bye!